Sisley

PARK
LANE

"The new is not found in the subject itself but in the manner of expressing it."

Camille Pissarro

Born the same year as Cézanne, Alfred Sisley was only a few years older than Renoir and Monet, and a few years younger than Degas and Manet. Although he was of English nationality, Sisley, at least physically, looked more like a Scandinavian, with blue eyes and a full beard. Yet of the group of painters who started the new independent movement that became known as the Impressionists, in spirit, he was the most French of them all.

More than any other, Sisley, in many of his innumerable works, has left us with the seductive and luminous memory of an Île-de-France bathed in light.

Alfred Sisley was born in 1839 in Paris, to English parents, and he would always remain, in Vaudoyer's words, "that Englishman who has become one of us", since his efforts to become a naturalised Frenchman, an enterprise attempted too late in life perhaps, did not end favourably.

His family, originally from Manchester, had established itself in France. His father William Sisley managed a business that exported artificial flowers to South America; his mother Felicia Sell came from a cultured London family. From her, Alfred developed a love of music and perhaps also from her, came his confident manner in society.

Sisley was sent to London from 1857 to 1861 for a commercial apprenticeship but it was not work that interested him. The sale of cotton or coffee captured his attention considerably less than his visits to the museums in England's capital city, where he delighted in the works of Constable, Bonington and Turner. The paintings of these landscapists from the English side of the Channel, whose love of light was combined with a taste for clean lines and a balanced composition, prefigured the future work of Alfred Sisley.

Upon his return to Paris in 1862, Sisley was given permission by his parents to abandon business and to dedicate himself exclusively to the study of art. Thus, in October that year, he enrolled in the studio of Charles-Marc-Gabriel Gleyre, a painter of Swiss origin whose work *Le Soir (illusions perdues)* had brought him sudden fame. There, Sisley met Frédéric Bazille, who became a life-long friend, as well as other young artists such as Monet and Renoir. Sisley's first works were sombre still-life paintings of glistening pikes from the Loing river, or game birds hanging from the wall or lying on a kitchen table, as in *The Pheasant*, the masterpiece of the Eugène Blot Collection of still-life paintings, whose colours remind one of those so beloved by Manet.

In those days, the art world was effervescent. Manet had just painted his *Déjeuner sur l'herbe* in 1863 and Sisley and his friends gathered around him to take part in that renaissance of French painting which was to become known as *Impressionism* (the name was originally given to the group derisively in 1874 following an exhibition of independent artists in the studio of the photographer Nadar, where Monet showed his eponymous work *Impression, Sunrise*).

For several months Sisley went daily to Gleyre's studio to copy live models. Once the young artist had learned the techniques of drawing, however, he realised very quickly that his ideas about landscapes would never have anything in common with those of his master. As Emile Montégut said in *Nos morts contemporains*, Gleyre "scarcely saw nature as anything except a setting and a background; for him, its only value was as an accessory". For Sisley, on the other hand, "a landscape was full of nuances, as full of quick changes of expression as

Woman with Umbrella, Summer - 1883.
Private collection, New York

a face...", as Gustave Geoffroy, a writer who became his friend late in life, expressed it. And in fact, the landscape was to become the keystone of Sisley's work.

Thus in the spring of 1863, along with his friends, Renoir, Monet and Bazille, Sisley left the Ecole des Beaux-Arts and went to paint directly out-of-doors in the forest at Fontainebleau.

For a time, he shared a studio with Auguste Renoir at Porte Maillot, 31 Avenue de Neuilly; then he moved to 15 Rue Moncey, and set up his own studio at 19 Rue de la Paix, finally settling down in Cité des Fleurs in Batignolles.

Every spring, however, Sisley and his friends returned to the Fontainebleau forests. There, they sometimes stayed in Chailly-en-Bière with Père Paillard at the Auberge du Cheval Blanc, and sometimes in Marlotte with Mère Anthony. It was there that Renoir, in 1868, painted the portrait of his friend Sisley and Sisley's young wife. In 1866, Sisley had married Eugénie Lescouezec, a native of Toul in the French province Meurthe et Moselle; they eventually had two children, Pierre and Jeanne.

When he was living in Paris, Sisley would often go to the Café

Guerbois, in the Grand-Rue des Batignolles, five minutes away from his studio in Cité des Fleurs, and there he would meet old classmates, from the Gleyre studio or from the Académie Suisse, gathered around Edouard Manet. He also met Emile Zola, who at the time was inseparable from his childhood friend Paul Cézanne, and others, like the painter Alfred Stevens, the draughtsman Constantin Guys, and the photographer Nadar.

Then, in 1870, Napoleon declared war on Prussia and contemporary society was turned upside-down.

Up until then, Sisley had only painted a few canvases. His father's fortune had allowed him to live a life of ease and as a result, he had enjoyed the luxury of remaining an amateur painter with no financial worries.

In those days, his palette was still dark and his treatment still polished and glossy. In his first landscapes, such as those of Marlotte and Celle-Saint-Cloud, for example, muted browns bordered dulled greens and blues, the clear result of a compromise between his instinct and his admiration for Courbet and Corot.

An example of Sisley's painting style in those early days was *Village Street in Marlotte* which today can be seen at the Albright Art Gallery in Buffalo, New York and also *View of Montmartre* which can be found in the Musée de Grenoble.

Beginning in 1870 the artist's style became freer, his palette grew lighter and in his work *Barges on the Canal Saint-Martin* painted that year, he adopted Impressionist techniques for the first time, using light colours and a chromatic division of light through dabs of juxtaposed colours. This was his first work in a long series of studies of river banks, which was interrupted only by his death.

His evolution continued until 1873 when, in his superb painting *The Seine at Daybreak, July 14th* he adopted Impressionist techniques without reserve. This progression was the result of a deep and conscious effort which the artist explained to the art critic Adolphe Tavernier in these terms: "Although the landscape painter should remain the master of his métier, the treatment should at certain times be more enthusiastic to express to the viewer the emotion that the artist has felt. You see that I am for a diversity of treatment in the same painting. This is not at all the current opinion but I think I am in the right especially when it is a matter of rendering an effect of light. For the sun, while it softens some parts of the landscape, plays up others, and these effects of light that are translated almost physically in nature should be rendered physically on canvas."

Unlike Renoir or even Degas, Sisley was only rarely attracted to portraiture. The few interior scenes that Sisley has left us are mostly of the kind where the presence of a model is incidental. An example is *The Lesson* where the painter has captured his son Pierre and his daughter Jeanne doing their homework on the dining room table. "Light", wrote Gustave Geoffroy, "softly animates the shadows, catches the sides of the vases, sings as it comes into contact with the flowers, gilds the cotton fringe below the mantle, lights up the waxed wood surface of the table, caresses the light-coloured smock of the schoolboy bending over his paper and catches the back of the girl's neck. Everything is silence, contemplation, study. One can almost hear the tick-tock of the alabaster clock."

The Franco-Prussian War had an adverse effect on the business affairs of William Sisley, Alfred's father. In 1871 the Sisley family was no longer able to sustain the heavy debts they had undertaken and were forced into bankruptcy. William Sisley died shortly thereafter. As a result, Alfred was no longer able to count on support from his family and from then on, he was forced to earn his living from painting.

During the Paris Commune, Sisley left that city and sought refuge in Voisin-Louveciennes, a village about thirty kilometres from the capital. There, he settled in a small house at 2 Rue de la Princesse, near the home of Renoir and his brother Edmond. From that village, Sisley often went with his friend to paint the countryside around the aque-

duct. And it was from there that on August 24th, 1871, an anguished Sisley watched Paris burn.

During the next four years in Louveciennes, Sisley tirelessly painted the peacefully flowing Seine with its banks bathed in light and a vast sky above, continuously reworking compositions. We should note at this point the importance of the sky in Sisley's works. Even his weaker canvases were saved by the striking manner in which he rendered the skies. In a letter to his friend, art critic Adolphe Tavernier, Sisley defined the role the sky played in his paintings thus: "Objects must be rendered with their own texture, especially if they are enveloped in light, as they are in nature. Here is where progress can be made. It is the sky that should be the means. The sky cannot be only a background. On the contrary, it contributes not only by giving depth to the planes (for the sky has different planes just like the land), but also by providing movement, by its form, and by its arrangement in rapport with the composition of the painting.

Is there anything more magnificent and more moving than that which one sees frequently in summer? I am speaking of the sky with its beautiful white wandering clouds. What movement! What allure, don't you think? It has the effect of waves when one is at the sea, it is exalting, it carries one away.

Another sky is the later evening sky. Its clouds are elongated, often taking the form of a ship's wake, of eddies that seem immobilised in the sky, and little by little, disappear, absorbed by the setting sun. It is the one that is the most tender, the most melancholy, with all the poignancy of things that vanish. It is the one I love particularly. But I don't want to tell you about all the skies that are dear to painters, I only want to tell you here about those that I prefer myself."

With their tranquil lines of vast skies and calm horizons, Sisley's paintings of the riverbanks of the Seine almost always have the same composition; that is, a few boats floating on the water, locks opened or closed in quiet villages, country lanes, and bridges reflected in the water. Everything is connected, everything is contained.

In 1872 in Paris, Sisley met Paul Durand-Ruel, an art dealer whose gallery was in the Rue Laffitte. Monet and Pissarro also knew him, having met him when they were living in London during the war, and it was they who introduced Sisley to Durand-Ruel.

The art dealer began to take an interest in Sisley and many of the other Impressionist painters as well, with whom he was developing his reputation and career, and through the difficult years, he became their champion.

Around this time, Sisley was working on his motif of the road seen in perspective, a theme which appeared for the first time perhaps in the well-known work of Hobbema *Middleharnis Lane*, which Sisley undoubtedly had admired at the National Gallery in London. It was a motif that was dear to other Impressionist painters such as Pissarro and Renoir as well.

In Sisley's work, the theme of the winding road would take on almost as much importance as that of the riverbanks. The road in perspective, often bordered by a row of trees, permitted him to express his passion for space, yet allowed him to retain the old composition, in which the sky occupied half the canvas. From April 15 to May 15th 1874, Sisley participated in the first exhibition held by the Impressionists (Société Anonyme Coopérative des Artistes peintres, sculpteurs, et graveurs) that the Batignolle group had decided to hold in opposition to the Salon, in the studio of the photographer Nadar at 35 Boulevard des Capucines.

Sisley exhibited five paintings there, two of which were *The Road to Saint-Germain* and *The Isle of the Loge*. Unfortunately, the exhibition was not a great success. In his book *Mémoires*, Paul Durand-Ruel wrote: "The public came in droves, but with their minds made up beforehand; they saw in these great artists only presumptuous fools trying to gain attention by their eccentricities. There was a wave of opinion against them and great hilarity, contempt and even indignation that permeated every circle, every studio, salon and even the theatres, where they were held up to ridicule."

Sisley did not sell a single painting and Durand-Ruel was forced, in spite of himself, to moderate his purchases. Since his father's death Sisley had had to support himself with his painting, and this lack of success threw him into a state of depression. The Café de la Nouvelle Athènes, Place Pigalle, became the new gathering place for the independent artists and Sisley went there often to forget his worries; it was there that he met such young artists as Franc-Lamy, Frédéric Cordey and Norbert Goetneutte.

During this period, the baritone Jean-Baptiste Faure, one of the foremost collectors of Impressionist works, invited Sisley to accompany him to Great Britain. The painter and his patron spent four months there and Sisley took advantage of his stay to paint some of his freshest and freest compositions. One of them was his *View from Charing Cross Bridge* in which, using an almost pointillist technique, Sisley strikingly captured the foggy London skies. He also painted views of the green banks of the Thames, the small town of Hampton Court and one, *The Molesey Regatta* from the old Caillebotte Collection, that precedes the compositions that Caillebotte himself painted several years later.

When he returned from England, Sisley left Louveciennes and moved to Marly-le-Roi. In an attempt to resolve their financial difficulties, Sisley, Renoir, Monet and Berthe Morisot decided to organise a sale by auction of their works. It was held on March 24th, 1875 at the Hôtel Drouot and, as might have been expected, it was a disaster. Albert Wolff, a critic for the newspaper *Figaro* described the artists as "monkeys who had gotten hold of palettes". In spite of help from a customs house official, Mr Victor Chocquet, who had become one of their staunchest supporters, they were unable to sell their paintings for the prices they hoped. The twenty-one canvases that Sisley put up for auction drew the paltry sum of only 2,440 francs.

Thus, in spite of this new exhibition, Sisley was still unable to solve his financial problems through the sale of his work.

At the second exhibition of the Independent Artists, held at the Durand-Ruel Gallery, 11 Rue Le Peletier, Sisley displayed eight canvases, and at the third such exhibit, he displayed seventeen, among them such masterpieces as *The Pit-Sawyers*, *The Argenteuil Bridge* and *The Machine of Marly*, but none of the canvases sold, no one talked about him, and even the press remained silent.

Far from letting this discourage him, however, Sisley found comfort in his music and his work and the strength to continue his pursuit in the quiet of his studio in Marly.

In 1877, Sisley moved with his family once again, this time to 7 Avenue de Bellevue in Sèvres.

There he set to work with new zeal, painting several views of the quays, the bridge and the roads of this small village as well as the famous porcelain factories. However, his financial situation grew worse, in spite of loans from his friend, the editor Georges Charpentier, and the help of a local baker Eugène Muret who organised a drawing in his shop to sell one of the artist's paintings. On August 18th, 1878, Sisley wrote to Théodore Duret to ask for his help. "Is there not someone among your friends of the Saintonge who is intelligent and has enough confidence in your artistic knowledge so that he could be convinced that he would be making a good investment by buying the works of a painter on the verge of success? If you know someone like that, here is what I would like to propose: 500 francs a month for six months, for thirty canvases. At the end of six months, as he will not want to keep thirty paintings by the same painter, he can select twenty of them, put them up for sale and get a return on his money of ten canvases for nothing ... For me it would be a matter of not letting the summer go by without working seriously, without worrying, and I could do some good work." But among his business contacts, Duret could only find one person willing to buy

seven canvases. This was Jourde, the publisher of *Siècle*.

In 1879, in the hope of finding new outlets for his work, Sisley decided that the time had come to exhibit at the Salon. But the Jury, predictably, refused his work. Tormented by poverty, the artist was forced to move yet again to another less expensive house. This time he moved to Veneux-Nadon near Moret. There he rendered the charm of that small sleepy village along the banks of the Loing, painting the Provencher windmill reflected in the river, the mills of the Marat at sunrise on winter mornings, and the arched stone bridge that straddled the Loing.

In June 1881 Sisley made a short visit to the Isle of Wight where the superb panoramas fascinated him, but the canvases he had ordered never arrived and so he left no pictorial record of that trip.

Back in France in September 1882 and wishing to be nearer to Moret, Sisley rented a house on the edge of the Fontainebleau forest.

Meanwhile, instead of improving, his financial situation was growing steadily more precarious. Selling his paintings became a constant preoccupation for him. On November 4th that year Sisley went with his friend Monet to see the art dealer Durand-Ruel to plan future group exhibitions. Monet's idea was "that individual exhibitions, one at a time, might be better for everyone than a group exhibition." Sisley, however, wrote to the art dealer on November 5th: "Past experience has shown that group exhibitions are most often successful and that individual exhibitions generally are not ... This does not seem to me to be the time for us to stop being nomads, have a place of our own, dream of inaugurating a new kind of exhibition and experiment. For me, our interest and yours is less one of showing lots of paintings than one of selling what we have. To reach this goal, a group exhibition, with a few paintings from each of us, will be much more effective and surely will be successful. That's how I feel about individual exhibitions."

But Durand-Ruel took Monet's advice and in the spring of 1883, organised five individual exhibitions, one after the other, for Boudin, Monet, Renoir, Pissarro and Sisley, in his gallery at 9 Boulevard de la Madeleine.

Sisley's turn began on June 1st, 1883, when he exhibited seventy paintings. It was a failure.

Four months later, Sisley moved once more to a house fifteen minutes from Moret, in Sablons, where he hoped to find a more gentle climate. From his stay in Sablons, the painter has left us many paintings of the riverbanks, a motif to which he never stopped returning, the banks of the Seine at Saint-Mammès, the dams of the Loing, the barges in the harbour, the hillsides of La Celle and the château of Croix-Blanche.

In 1889, he returned with his family to Moret-sur-Loing, first to Rue de l'Eglise in the centre of the little medieval village, then to a small house surrounded by a garden on the corner of Rue du Château and Rue Montmartre where he stayed for the rest of his life.

In 1889, the year of the Paris World's Fair in the Champs-de-Mars, the Société des Artistes Français held its Salon. In opposition to that society, the Société Nationale des Beaux-Arts was formed, and in February 1890, it admitted Sisley, as an associate member, to its exhibitions. So, from May 15th to May 30th of that year, Sisley participated for the first time in the exhibition of the Société Nationale. He displayed six landscapes which were favourably received. From that moment on, except for two years, 1896 and 1897, the artist participated in this exhibition every year, although with an ever decreasing number of paintings.

It was from this last period that his "series" date. These were works with the same motif painted at different times of the day, to capture the changing light and seasons. The banks of the Loing bordered with poplars, the footpaths in Sablons, the old houses of Saint-Mammès and the hillsides of La Celle-sous-Moret were some of his favourite themes. In this series, painted in the last years of his career, the vision of the artist was transformed and became more systematic; the masses of greenery, for example, were often rendered by a new grating green. However, what his paintings gained in force, they lost in clearness. Speaking of series, a special mention must be made of some fifteen paintings that the artist finished between 1894 and 1895. These were of the church in Moret, portrayed almost always without perspective and taking up three-quarters of the canvas; Sisley's churches remind one of Monet's paintings of the Cathedral in Rouen – a comparison that is not without foundation as the two friends had agreed to study, each in his own way, the variations of light on the façades of old churches. Even though he seldom travelled far from that region, Sisley did make one trip to Normandy in 1894 and in the spring of 1897, two years before his death, he went for the last time to England. He was able to see an old wish come true, that of returning once again to the place from which his family had come, thanks to the generosity of François Depeaux, an industrialist from Rouen and a patron. Depeaux, who had to go to London on business, not only invited Sisley to accompany him but also paid for Sisley's stay for four months on the other side of the Channel, buying in advance several canvases that the artist would paint while there.

After visiting London and stopping in the south of England, Sisley decided to spend time in Penarth, in Wales. There he painted several seascapes of the cliffs of Langland, near Swansea and of Cardiff, Lady's Cove and Storr Rock. He described his visit to his friend Gustave Geoffroy: "I have been here eight days after taking a train journey through the south of England and spending three days in Falmouth in Cornwall. I am resting a bit after that somewhat tiring journey before beginning my work. The countryside is pretty and the harbour with its big ships entering and leaving Cardiff is superb ... I don't know how long I will stay in Penarth, I am very comfortable here, staying *in lodgings* with kind people. The climate is very gentle, very warm these days, in fact, even at this very moment as I write you. I expect to get as much as I can from what I see around me and be back in the good village of Moret towards the month of October." That same year 1897, in February, the art dealer Georges Petit organised a complete retrospective of Sisley's work in his gallery at 8 Rue Sèze. It was a very fine exhibition of forty-six paintings and six pastels, but the press did not like it and Sisley sold nothing. It was the coup de grâce. At the end of his life, Sisley decided to sort out the problem of his nationality, for even though he had retained his English citizenship until then, his heart was in France, especially in the Île-de-France. Unfortunately it was a decision made too late and, having lost certain necessary papers, the painter who, more than any of the other Impressionists, had rendered the sweetness of the Île-de-France countryside, died a citizen of Albion.

On October 8th, 1898, already consumed with cancer, Sisley suffered the loss of his beloved wife and lifelong companion.

The artist fell apart. Sisley spent his last days alone, in both physical and spiritual pain.

Sensing that death was near, Sisley called upon his old friend Claude Monet to look after his two children and on January 29th, 1899, he died. Ironically, it was only then that success, denied him throughout his life, arrived. Three months after his death, the art dealers with a desperate eagerness, sold every one of the canvases left in his studio.

Moret-sur-Loing - 1892. Private collection, Paris

1. Portrait of Alfred Sisley - Auguste Renoir - 1874. The Art Institute of Chicago. Mr. and Mrs. Lewis L. Colburn Memorial Collection - *Renoir first met Sisley in Gleyre's studio where Alfred enrolled after his return from England in October 1862. The two became inseparable friends. When Renoir painted this portrait, the two artists had just participated in the first Impressionist exhibition held in the studio of the photographer Nadar.*

2. The Pheasant - 1867-68. Private collection, New York - *The few still life paintings that Sisley did, date mainly from the early years of his career. He has left a few paintings of fish, such as luminous-scaled pike from the river Loing and a few of game birds, as in this sombre composition. The subtle colours of the pheasant resting on an unadorned tressle table recall the shades beloved by Manet.*

3. Village Street in Marlotte - 1866. The Albright Art Gallery, Buffalo, New York - *Each spring, Sisley, Renoir and other Impressionists went to work out-of-doors in the forests of Fontainebleau. They often stayed at Mère Anthony's in Marlotte. This work, characterised by its sombre palette, shows the influence of the masters of the Barbizon group.*

4. Lane with Chestnut Trees, La-Celle-Saint-Cloud - 1865. Musée du Petit Palais, Paris - *When Sisley painted this scene, his palette was still sombre and his canvases had the polished smooth surfaces found in his first landscapes of La-Celle-Saint-Cloud. In these paintings, muted browns lie next to deep greens, a clear attempt at compromise between his instincts and his admiration for Courbet and Corot.*

5. Game Warden in the Fontainebleau Forest - 1870. Private collection, New York - *In this painting of a game warden crossing a clearing in the Fontainebleau forest, one can find hints of what would become Impressionist technique in the treatment of sunlight and its effect on greenery. The zones of light and shadow are well-distributed here, giving a feeling of space.*

6. The Lesson - 1871. Private collection, Paris - *Unlike his friend and fellow artist, Auguste Renoir, portraiture only rarely attracted Sisley, and although he sometimes painted interior scenes, they were more often genre paintings in which the presence of the models was secondary. Here the painter has captured his children, Pierre and Jeanne, as they do their homework on the dining room table.*

7. The Seine at Argenteuil - 1872. Richard J. Bernhard Foundation, New York - *Throughout his life, Sisley tirelessly painted many similar compositions that had, as their theme, the peacefully flowing Seine, with its river banks bathed in sunlight under a vast blue sky. In his canvases, Sisley gave the sky a prominent role, wishing to "envelope it with light as it is in nature."*

8. Barges on the Canal Saint-Martin - 1870. Oskar Reinhart am Römerholz Collection, Wintherthur - *Beginning in 1870, Sisley's style become freer, his palette grew lighter. In this work, he adopted for the first time what would become Impressionist techniques, that is, the use of lighter colours and a chromatic division of light through the use of spots of colours, juxtaposed.*

9. Square at Argenteuil - 1872. Musée du Louvre, Paris - *Between 1872 and 1874, Sisley created some of his most sensitive paintings. Like Corot, Sisley loved to paint the play of light on old stone. In this village square in Argenteuil, the yellow and white façades are painted without dryness, and show a concern for minor details. Note the subtle gradations of tones so that the green shutters become bluer in the shadows.*

10. The Village on the Edge of the Woods, Autumn - 1872. Private collection, Paris - *In this work, Sisley gave the landscape a place of honour and was able to render the intense emotion that a landscape can produce at certain times of the year. Here, the almost bare trees reveal a sky that, as the painter said, "can only be a background" offering "depth by its planes... and movement by its form, by its arrangement in rapport with the tableau's composition."*

11. The Seine at Argenteuil - 1872. Private collection, Lausanne - *The compositions Sisley chose when he painted the banks of the Seine were almost always the same. There are vast skies occupying half the canvas, calm horizons, and boats floating on the water near peaceful villages. Better than anyone else, Sisley was able to capture the charm and sweetness of the Île-de-France.*

12. A Corner of Louveciennes - 1872. Private collection, Paris - *During the Paris Commune, Sisley left that city and sought refuge in Voisin-Louveciennes, a village some thirty kilometres from the capital. There, he lived in a small house near his friend Auguste Renoir. He stayed for four years. From that period, he left a large quantity of paintings that had as their theme the village and its surroundings.*

13. Road at Louveciennes - 1874. Musée d'Orsay, Paris - *Sisley was not only attracted by the countryside in summer; he often found his effects in snow-covered views, rendering with great mastery the gossamer-like snow that enveloped the houses in a fleecy blanket. The painter lived in the house on the right for a few months.*

14. Louveciennes, the Sèvres Road - 1873. Musée du Louvre, Paris - *In Louveciennes Sisley worked on the motif of the road, seen in perspective. The first painting with that theme may have been Hobbema's famous "Middleharnis Lane", which Sisley had come across during a visit to the National Gallery in London. The theme of the winding road was also taken up by other Impressionist painters such as Pissarro and Renoir.*

15. Snow, Louveciennes - 1874. Courtauld Institute, London - *In this painting Sisley again takes up the motif of the winding road, in an attempt to express his passionate interest in the portrayal of space. His palette shows great sobriety and perfect balance; the slightest nuances of light are noted without creating an abstraction of forms.*

16. An Inn at Hampton Court - 1874. Private collection, Zurich - *During his stay in England, at the invitation of the baritone Jean-Baptiste Faure, one of the first collectors of the works of the Impressionists, Sisley painted some of his freshest and freest compositions, such as this view of the small village of Hampton Court.*

17. The Bridge at Hampton Court - 1874. Wallraf-Richartz Museum, Cologne - *Like the preceding work, this canvas dates from the second trip Sisley made with his patron Faure to England, where he spent four months. This painting of the Thames with its green riverbanks, has a composition which is similar to many others. Sisley found the little village of Hampton Court with its iron bridge, its shady lanes and its tranquil footpaths along the river particularly attractive.*

18. July 14th at Marly-le-Roi - 1875. Lady Baillie Collection, London - *On his return from England, Sisley left Louveciennes and moved to the solitude of Marly where he painted innumerable works. He did a series on the floods at Port-Marly, and this "July 14th" whose theme of the decked-out holiday streets is rendered with subtle touches to capture the poetry of that peaceful celebration.*

19. View of the Thames and Charing Cross Bridge - 1874. Baron Louis de Chollet Collection, Friburg - *In this canvas, Sisley was able to translate forcefully, with short, almost pointillist strokes, the foggy, smog-filled sky of the English capital and the muted effect of light on the surface of the Thames. This fresh composition dates from Sisley's second stay in England with his patron, the baritone Jean-Baptiste Faure.*

20. First Frost - 1876. Private collection, New York - *In his landscapes, Sisley searched for a certain organisation of space, a certain sense of construction that linked him to Corot and led him to respect the relationships between the different planes. The road leading to the horizon was one of his favourite themes. He used it to link the foreground with the background of a composition, for it allowed him to work with the idea of space and helped create his refined effects of perspective.*

21. Still Life, Apples and Grapes - 1876. The Sterling and Francine Clark Art Institute, Williamstown. Mass. - *Among Sisley's works, there are only three or four still life paintings in total. This one, of apples and grapes, has a subtle harmony of colours and shapes, painted with quick broken strokes. It precedes the paintings Bonnard would do some thirty years later.*

22. Banks of the Seine at Bougival - 1876. Private collection, New York - *In this landscape of the Île-de-France, dating from the time when he lived in Marly-le-Roi, poetic magic is rendered in only a few elements, earth, sky and water, united by the luminous vibrations of light. Sisley often tried to humanise his landscapes, as in this canvas, by painting in small figures in the manner of Jongkind.*

23. Snow at Marly-le-Roi - 1875. Musée du Louvre, Paris - *Sisley's landscapes approach those of Pissarro or Monet. But Sisley's works have a resonance that is more intimate, more tender and yet also more restless. The brilliant chromatic burst of so many of the Impressionist painters is subdued in Sisley as he creates his silent atmosphere. As in this elegiac landscape, a field covered in snow or a flooded road were subjects that fascinated him.*

24. Snow at Louveciennes - 1878. Musée d'Orsay, Paris - *The theme of snow often attracted the Impressionists for it gave them an excuse to study the effects of variations of light. Touches of broken colour gave the illusion of a uniform white background with mottled blue reflections. For Sisley, like Courbet, the winter countryside always held a particular charm; its silence more closely reflected Sisley's own temperament than the sunny landscapes that Renoir so loved.*

25. The Flood at Port-Marly - 1876. Musée d'Orsay, Paris - *This is the most famous tableau of a series of six on the same theme. The dominant colours are the grey-blue nuances of the sky reflected in the water, interrupted by the three horizontal bands of the hotel, painted in lively tones. Silhouettes in the manner of Jongkind enliven this landscape, and the composition of the painting takes on a serene note in spite of the tragic event it depicts.*

26. The Boat in the Flood - 1876. Musée d'Orsay, Paris - *Like the previous work this one comes from the Camondo collection. However, it is smaller in size and Sisley has chosen to paint it from a slightly different point of view which, according to P. Jamot, was "the first idea for the final composition". A year after Sisley's death, this work was put on sale from the critic Tavernier's collection; it was the first of Sisley's paintings to sell for a high price.*

27. Farmyard, Saint-Mammès - 1884. Musée du Louvre, Paris - *The artist had just moved to Sèvres when he painted this work. Sisley did not seek out unusual scenes or exceptional sky lines. The compositions of his canvases were limited to only a few things: a simple farmyard with trodden ground and the sky showing above the rooftops were sufficient to portray the somewhat antiquated charm of the French province.*

28. The Old Ferry Path - c. 1880. The Tate Gallery, London - *The year 1880 marked the great changes in the work of Sisley. During that period, the artist often painted the banks of the Loing, a small tributary of the Seine. The structure of the tableau is original. The painter chose a cove of the river where he could see the opposite shore through the poplars. Sisley wrote the critic Tavernier: "I always begin a canvas with the sky."*

29. A View of the Sèvres - 1879. Private collection, Paris - *The same year, 1879, Sisley decided to submit some paintings to the Salon so that his work might become better known and new channels might be opened to the artist, but the jury refused his canvases. The artist went back to work, tirelessly painting the Sèvres countryside where he had just moved. In this canvas, he returned to the theme of the winding road so dear to the Impressionists.*

30. The Dinghy at Veneux, September Afternoon - 1882. Private collection, New York - *Refused by the Salon and struggling with poverty, Sisley was forced to look for less expensive lodgings. He found them in Veneux-Nadon near Moret where he was able to continue working. There he portrayed the charm of that small sleepy village along the banks of the Loing. In this canvas, he has added the silhouette of a young woman in the foreground.*

31. The Tug-boat - 1877. Musée du Petit Palais, Paris - *Sisley left Marly-le-Roi in 1877 and moved to Sèvres where a local tradesman Murer organised a lottery of Sisley's paintings in his shop, in an attempt to help the artist out of his financial difficulties. Once again, earth, sky and water are combined with a few small figures, painted in the manner of Jongkind.*

32. Old Houses in Saint-Mammès, Autumn - 1880. Private collection, Paris - *More than sun-filled landscapes, Sisley preferred the softened shades of spring and autumn, as in this canvas with its reddish tones, where even the sky seems to reflect the colour of the dead leaves and the old stones. Sisley was very fond of Saint-Mammès, a village where the Loing enters the Seine, and he left many canvases from his stay there.*

33. The Loing and the Church at Moret - 1888. Mr and Mrs. David M. Heyman Collection, New York - *Sisley had studied in depth the works of Corot and the painters of the Barbizon group, as well as the Dutch landscape painters of the seventeenth century. Following the example of Ruysdael who devoted a large part of his composition to the sky, Sisley has accentuated its importance here.*

34. The Last Leaves of Autumn - 1883. Mr and Mrs Joseph Rosensaft Collection, New York - *In the short strokes of juxtaposed colour under an almost flaming sky, seen through the rust-colours leaves of the tree, Sisley has captured the charm and poetry of France as described by the sixteenth century French poet Joachim du Bellay.*

35. The Bridge and Mills of Moret in Summer - 1888. Mr Grégoire C. Sazlmanowitz Collection, Geneva - *Around 1888, the small village of Moret with its gates and belfries, its lanes and small houses dominated by the church bell became one of Sisley's favourite motifs. In this summer landscape, the artist has portrayed the Loing river reflecting on its surface the Provencher mill and the Moret bridge with its stone arches.*

36. Moret-sur-Loing, the Bridge, the Church and the Mills - 1892. Private collection, Paris - *This view of Moret was often portrayed by Sisley at different hours of the day as the light and the seasons changed. This motif became a true series in which the bridge over the Loing and the Provencher mill always played important roles.*

37. The Tannery Road at Moret - 1892. Private collection, Paris - *Some of Sisley's most vibrant works were of the little medieval village of Moret. In this canvas, the artist has brought to life the little street where the tannery was located, giving its sleepy houses, under an early afternoon sun, a calm animation.*

38. Saint-Mammès - 1885. Private collection, New York - *The banks of the Loing bordered with poplars, the sandy paths, the old houses of Saint-Mammès and the hillsides of La Celle-sous-Moret were Sisley's favourite motifs in his last period. In this work, with its glowing composition, we see once again the importance of the sky to the artist.*

39. The Church of Notre Dame at Moret in Sunshine - 1893. Musée des Beaux-Arts, Rouen - *Among the series painted by Sisley, special mention must be made of some fifteen works the artist painted from 1893 to 1895 of the church of Moret. It was almost always portrayed from the same point of view, without perspective, and its imposing mass takes up three-quarters of the canvas.*

40. The Church at Moret, Afternoon - 1895. Private collection, Lausanne - *One often links the series of churches painted by Sisley with the cathedral of Rouen painted time and time again by Monet. It is a comparison not without foundation, for the two friends had thought of studying, each in his own way, the variations of light on the façades of old churches.*

41. The Canal of the Loing - 1892. Musée d'Orsay, Paris - *This is one of the many canvases with the same theme that was offered to the Musée du Luxembourg in 1899, thanks to a gift from the friends of the artist, which was organised by Monet. The structure of the composition is original and the perspective recalls the motif of the winding road leading to the horizon.*

42. Thatched Cottage in Normandy - 1894. Private collection, Paris - *In summer 1894, Sisley stayed in Normandy as the guest of the industrialist François Depeaux, at his home in Mesnil-Esnard outside Rouen. At the request of his host, Sisley painted several canvases of the meadows of Sahurs along the Seine and the Normandy farms along the slopes of the Bouille.*

43. Storr Rock, Lady's Cove, Evening - 1897. Private collection, New York - *During his stay in Penarth, Sisley painted several seascapes with similar motifs. In this composition, the enormous boulder against which waves are breaking gave the artist the opportunity to study the luminous vibrations of the sea.*

44. The Banks of the Seine: Gust of Wind - 1894. Musée des Beaux-Arts, Rouen - *Many of Sisley's works had similar compositions and we can compare the structure of this work with his painting "The Loing and the Church of Moret" dated 1888, where the different planes are similar but placed so they seem to reflect each other.*

1. *Portrait of Alfred Sisley* - Auguste Renoir, 1874. The Art Institute of Chicago,
Mr and Mrs.Lewis L. Colburn Memorial Collection

2. *The Pheasant* - 1867-68. Private collection, New York

3. *Village Street in Marlotte* - 1866. The Albright Art Gallery, Buffalo, New York

4. *Lane with Chestnut Trees, La-Celle-Saint-Cloud* - 1865. Musée du Petit Palais, Paris

5. *Game Warden in the Fontainebleau Forest* - 1870.
   Private collection, New York

6. *The Lesson* - 1871. Private collection, Paris

7. *The Seine at Argenteuil* - 1872. Richard J. Bernhard Foundation, New York

8. *Barges on the Canal Saint-Martin* - 1870. Oskar Reinhart
am Römerholz Collection, Wintherthur

9. *Square at Argenteuil* - 1872. Musée du Louvre, Paris

10. *The Village on the Edge of the Woods, Autumn* - 1872. Private collection, Paris

11. *The Seine at Argenteuil* - 1872. Private collection, Lausanne

12. *A Corner of Louveciennes* - 1872. Private collection, Paris

13. *Road at Louveciennes* - 1874. Musée d'Orsay, Paris

14. *Louveciennes, the Sèvres Road* - 1873. Musée du Louvre, Paris

15. *Snow, Louveciennes* - 1874. Courtauld Institute, London

16. *An Inn at Hampton Court* - 1874. Private collection, Zurich

17. *The Bridge at Hampton Court* - 1874. Wallraf-Richartz Museum, Cologne

18. *July 14th at Marly-le-Roi* - 1875. Lady Baillie Collection, London

19. *View of the Thames and Charing Cross Bridge* - 1874. Baron Louis de Chollet Collection, Friburg

20. *First Frost* -1876. Private collection, New York

21. *Still-Life, Apples and Grapes* - 1876.
The Sterling and Francine Clark Art Institute, Williamstown, Mass.

22. *Banks of the Seine at Bougival* - 1876. Private collection, New York

23. *Snow at Marly-le-Roi* - 1875. Musée du Louvre, Paris

24. *Snow at Louveciennes* - 1878. Musée d'Orsay, Paris

25. *The Flood at Port-Marly* - 1876. Musée d'Orsay, Paris

26. *The Boat in the Flood* - 1876. Musée d'Orsay, Paris

27. *Farmyard, Saint-Mammès* - 1884. Musée du Louvre, Paris

28. *The Old Ferry Path* - 1880. The Tate Gallery, London

29. *A View of the Sèvres* - 1879. Private collection, Paris

30. *The Dinghy at Veneux, September Afternoon* - 1882. Private collection, New York

31. *The Tug-boat* - 1877. Musée du Petit Palais, Paris

32. *Old Houses in Saint-Mammès, Autumn* - 1880. Private collection, Paris

33. *The Loing and the Church at Moret* - 1888. Mr. and Mrs. David M. Heyman Collection, New York

34. *The Last Leaves of Autumn* - 1883.
   Mr. and Mrs. Joseph Rosensaft Collection, New York

35. *The Bridge and Mills of Moret in Summer* - 1888. Mr.Grégoire C. Sazlmanowitz Collection, Geneva

36. *Moret-sur-Loing, the Bridge, the Church and the Mills* - 1892. Private collection, Paris

37. *The Tannery Road at Moret* - 1892. Private collection, Paris

38. *Saint-Mammès* - 1885. Private collection, New York

39. *The Church of Notre Dame at Moret in Sunshine* - 1893. Musée des Beaux-Arts, Rouen

40. *The Church at Moret, Afternoon* - 1895. Private collection, Lausanne

41. *The Canal of the Loing* - 1892. Musée d'Orsay, Paris

2. *Thatched Cottage in Normandy* - 1894. Private collection, Paris

43. *Storr Rock, Lady's Cove, Evening* - 1897. Private collection, New York

44. *The Banks of the Seine: Gust of Wind* - 1894. Musée des Beaux-Arts, Rouen

Editor in chief Anna Maria Mascheroni

Art director Luciano Raimondi

Text Alberta Melanotte

Translation Kerry Milis

Production Art, Bologna

Photo Credits Gruppo Editoriale Fabbri S.p.A., Milan

Copyright © 1988 by Gruppo Editoriale S.p.A., Milan

Published by Park Lane
An imprint of Books & Toys Limited
The Grange
Grange Yard
LONDON
SE1 3AG

ISBN 1-85627-106-4

This edition published 1991

Printed in Italy by Gruppo Editoriale Fabbri S.p.A., Milan